Estate Planning – How to Protect Everything You Have for Everyone You Love

The Basics of Estate Planning in Alabama

Bill Miller, JD

ISBN: 9781519650719
ISBN 13: 9781505698848
Library of Congress Control Number: 2014922729
LCCN Imprint Name: **City and State (If applicable)**

Contents

Why I Wrote This Book

This Book Is Not Legal Advice

Introduction

Chapter 1: What Is a Will?

Chapter 2: What Is a Power of Attorney?

Chapter 3: What Is an Advanced Medical Directive?

Chapter 4: What Is Probate?

Chapter 5: What Is a Trust and Why Use Trust-Based Planning?

Chapter 6: Asset Protection: You Must Know Your Creditors and Predators

Chapter 7: Long-Term Care: How Will I Pay?

Chapter 8: Applying for Medicaid

Chapter 9: Other Issues

Chapter 10: Why Miller Estate and Elder Law?

Register for Free Workshops

Estate Planning Workshop: *7 Biggest Mistakes People Make in Estate Planning and How to Avoid Them*

Introduction

Have you ever had questions or concerns about any of the following?

- o Who gets your property in the event you die unexpectedly?

- o What would happen to your property if you suddenly became incapacitated or incompetent?

- o What happens to your assets in the event you have to go into a nursing home?

- o What if you are in an accident and have to be put on life support?

- o How will the doctors know whether you want to die or be on life support?

- o If you give money to your children or grandchildren, will you have to pay a gift tax on the money?

o If you give away assets, will that disqualify you from Medicaid in the event you have to go into a nursing home?

If you have ever asked one or more of these questions, you are not alone. These are some of the most common questions we are asked. Many people think that estate planning and asset protection is only for the very wealthy. Nothing could be further from the truth.

You have spent your entire life accumulating assets and reaping the rewards of your hard work. Don't you think it is worth some investment of time to determine what your options are in the event you die prematurely, become incapacitated and need someone else to act on your behalf, or have to go into a nursing home?

All estate planning comes down to three basic questions:

1. Who is in control of my assets?

2. Who gets to benefit from my assets/money?

3. When?

Obviously, when you are alive and well, you are in control, and you get to decide who benefits. But what happens if you have a stroke or develop dementia or some other health problem, and you are no longer able to manage your own care or your stuff. Now who is in control? Who is in charge of your care? Who controls your stuff? Who benefits from your stuff, and who should not benefit? Who should make these decisions? The State of Alabama? You? Someone else?

What if you die? Now who is in control of your stuff? Who benefits from your stuff? What if your spouse remarries?

All of these issues have to do with estate planning.

Do I need a will? Do I need a trust? How do I know if I need both? This book provides the answers to those questions in a very general sense. However, no one can properly advise you until you meet with an attorney who is qualified to answer these questions and who knows how to prepare a plan that satisfies your needs and desires.

If you do not put your own plan in place, the State of Alabama has a plan for you. This choice comes down to whether you want your own plan or whether you want to use the state's plan. If you fail to plan, your family will have to deal with the difficulty of making decisions about what to do about you and your money when something happens to you. Don't leave that heavy burden on them. Learn how easy it is to put a plan in place to protect everything you have for everyone you love.

Chapter 1

What Is a Will?

A will is a legal document that you draft that determines who gets your assets that are in your probate estate at the time of your death. Most people have heard of a will, and many people have one. A will is only effective upon your death and only covers the disposition of assets that are in your probate estate at the time of your death.

Your probate estate consists of only those assets that are in your name at the time of your death. Those assets may include land, IRA's, stocks, automobiles, CDs, or cash in accounts in your name. Many times people are unaware when they make a will how they own their assets. For example, most bank accounts with more than one person on the account are set up as survivorship accounts. When you die, the surviving person on the account owns the account immediately, even if you put all the money in the account. It never becomes part of your probate estate, and therefore the will is not relevant to that asset. When preparing a will, it is important to look at how you own the asset to be sure the will is effective to achieve your intent.

When you draft a will, you name each person who you want to receive specific assets, or you detail how you want to divide your assets in general. You will also name the person who is to handle your estate at the time of your death. That person is known as an executor or executrix. You will also have to decide whether you want the executor to post a bond and to file an inventory of your assets at the time of your death.

If you do not have a will when you pass away and you have assets that are still in your name, then someone will have to file in probate court to handle your estate. Alabama law requires the person to post a bond, file an inventory, and file an accounting of all of the assets that have been handled. The state has rules as to who gets what assets. This can be very complicated if you have children by a prior marriage or other family issues. The state's rules are known as intestate succession, and they set out the disposition of your property, whether it was the way you wanted it or not. Additionally, administration of an estate without a will is usually much more expensive and time-consuming than probating an estate with a will. The bond itself requires that a premium be paid. The amount of the bond depends on the value of the estate. The administrator has to pay the initial premium out of his own pocket up front and then get reimbursed from the estate several months down the road. Filing an inventory of assets entails going into the home, listing all personal property, figuring out all of the financial assets and their location, and so forth. These activities are tedious and time-consuming and can be waived in a will.

Chapter 2

What Is a Power of Attorney?

A power of attorney is a legal document that gives someone else authority to act legally on your behalf. A power of attorney can be very broad and general, or it can be very specific. An example of a specific power of attorney is when you buy a car and need to put the title in your name; you give the dealership power of attorney to transfer the title over to you. That is the only power that is given to the dealership. You can give a very broad power of attorney, which allows someone else to sign documents, access your bank accounts, pay bills, and do any other legal act that you authorize them to do. A power of attorney is broader than a blank check. If I give you a blank check, the most you can take from me is what is in my checking account. If I give you a broad power of attorney, you can take everything I have. Therefore, it is important that whomever you name as your power of attorney is someone who you know and trust.

Spouses commonly give each other an immediate power of attorney that is very broad. You can also give a springing power of attorney, which is a power of attorney that does not go into effect until certain criteria are met, such as two doctors indicating that you are incompetent or incapacitated and no longer able to handle your legal affairs. A springing power of attorney is not activated until the specific conditions are met.

Again, if you do not have a power of attorney, the state determines what happens in the event you become incapacitated or incompetent and need someone to act on your behalf. If you become incapacitated or incompetent, then someone has to go to probate court and file a petition for conservatorship and guardianship. A guardianship is the legal authority to determine what happens to you, and a conservatorship is the legal authority to determine what happens to your property. Everything thereafter is subject to reporting to and approval by the court. A guardianship and conservatorship proceeding is much more expensive and time-consuming than executing a power of attorney. The person who is appointed as guardian or conservator has to report their actions to the court on a regular basis and in some cases get court approval prior to acting. A durable power of attorney prevents this necessity and allows the person you choose and trust to act immediately.

We had a client once who came to see us in a panic. His ex-wife, who was in her mid-forties, had suffered a bad stroke and was in the hospital. They had two teenage boys, ages seventeen and fifteen. The ex-wife had no other family. The doctors informed the boys that their mother would have to go to a nursing home for the rest of her life. Unfortunately, the mother did not have a power of attorney. As a result, no one was legally authorized to act on her behalf; no one could pay her bills, cash her checks, access her bank accounts, and so forth.

We had to file with the probate court for a guardianship and conservatorship. Obviously, the court was reluctant to name an ex-spouse as the person legally authorized to act on behalf of the boys' mother. The boys were too young to legally make decisions. The father was not very excited about having to do it either. He had to spend his time and money to manage the mother's money and decide where to put her for care.

We eventually got a good friend of the mother's to serve as guardian and conservator. If the mother had created a power of attorney, we could have saved a lot of time, money, and heartache because she could have named the friend and given that friend very specific instructions as to how to manage her money and any health care crisis that came up. This is an example of how threats number four and five can be devasting. Her health failed when she did not expect it and she had not planned for it in advance.

Chapter 3

What Is an Advanced Medical Directive?

Most people by now have heard of advanced medical directives and living wills. These are legal documents in which you determine ahead of time what types of life-sustaining treatment you want in the event you become incapacitated. For example, if you have a stroke or are in a bad accident and can only remain alive on a ventilator or respirator, then you could give directions in advance not to be placed on those machines. There are two parts to an advanced medical directive: a living will and a medical power of attorney. Having an advanced medical directive with specific instructions can save your family members a great deal of pain and heartache.

In addition to stating your wishes about end-of-life scenarios in the living will, you can also name a medical power of attorney who can help make decisions about the end of life for you. The two parts work together. Without a medical power of attorney, the doctors make decisions about anything that is not covered adequately in your living will. It is very difficult to plan for every contingency in a living will. The medical power of attorney can give the person you designate very limited or expanded authority to make medical decisions for you if you cannot make them for yourself. The medical power of attorney goes along with your living will but allows a loved one to make decisions for you instead of the doctors or the court.

If you do not have an advanced directive and wind up on life support or on a breathing machine, the State of Alabama has rules as to what happens and whether you remain on life support. Nowadays, when you go into a hospital, they almost always ask if you have an advanced directive. If you do not have one, they have a generic advanced directive form and will ask you to sign it. The problem is that it is drafted by the hospital's attorneys and is designed to protect the hospital. It is not designed to protect you or to be specific about your interests and desires should that need arise.

The story of Terry Schaivo from Florida is a common example of what happens to families when a person becomes incapacitated without an advanced directive. Briefly, Terry Schaivo was comatose and incompetent for several years. Her parents and husband could not agree on whether she wanted to remain on life support and be fed through a breathing tube. Sadly, the situation turned very bad, and the parties fought in court for months at great expense. There were several appeals before the Supreme Court finally decided the case.

A well-drafted advanced medical directive is an essential tool in your estate plan. It makes no difference how much money you have. A good advanced medical directive will make it much easier on your loved ones and also ensure that your wishes are carried out. Everyone has different wishes. As an example, we had a client who had two sons. She named one as her medical power of attorney, and in her advanced directive, she was very specific that she did not want any family to visit her in the nursing home if she had Alzheimer's. She did not want her family to remember her that way. Those were her wishes. The other son had a hard time with it but had to abide by her rules because she had set them out ahead of time in her advanced medical directive. Not having an advanced directive can cause confusion and disagreement for your family members which leads to pain and heartache.

Chapter 4

What Is Probate?

Probate is the process of administering someone's estate after they pass away. As mentioned in chapter 1, if you have a will, the probate process will follow your directions as set out in your will. Without a will, the probate process is known as an administration of an estate and will follow the rules set out by the State of Alabama.

Assuming you have a will when you die, your executor takes your will to the probate court, files it, and requests what is called letters testamentary. Letters testamentary are letters or documents that authorize your executor to act legally on behalf of your estate. Once the letters testamentary are issued, the executor can collect all of your assets, pay your creditors, dispurse your assets to the appropriate heirs, and close the estate. That all sounds much simpler than it actually is.

In order for your executor to be approved, all of your potential heirs have to get notice and agree that person should serve as the executor. People are often reluctant to sign affidavits. We have people come into our office all the time who do not want to sign, wonder why they have to sign, or question whether they are giving up their rights. The problem is that any of these roadblocks along the way cause delays in the legal process. If you do not have a will, the process takes even longer.

The probate process takes, at a minimum, seven to nine months. Again, that assumes that there are no hurdles along the way. If one of the potential heirs objects or does not agree at any point in time, then the probate court has to have a hearing. That obviously increases the time and expense to the estate. If you have a child who is underage or disabled, then the court has to appoint a guardian *ad litem* (attorney appointed by the court to represent and protect the interests of a person who cannot legally protect his or her own interests due to incompetency or age) for that heir, which also costs the estate more legal fees and time. If you cannot find a potential heir, then he or she has to be served by publication in a local newspaper. Service by publication takes at least three weeks, and that service has to happen every time there is a hearing!

It is also important to know that everything about probate is public. Anyone can go to the probate court and request the file regarding your estate to see how much money you had at the time you died, what assets you left to whom, how much debt you had, or who your creditors were at the time of your death. In addition to probate being a public process, it can be expensive. The most recent study by the AARP indicates that the cost to probate an estate that is not contested is somewhere between 5 percent and 20 percent of the value of the estate. We have had heirs contact us on many occasions and ask what they need to do to contest a will. Because the probate process requires that all potential heirs sign documents agreeing to the disposition as set out in the will, a potential heir can simply refuse to sign one of those documents and thereby create a will contest by doing nothing. A will contest prolongs the process and increases the expense drastically.

As mentioned previously, a will only governs the assets in your probate estate. Therefore, any asset that passed outside your probate estate is not covered. For example, if you own an asset jointly with another person and you pass away, then that asset will transfer to the surviving person. You can also have beneficiary-designated assets such as IRAs, 401(k)s, life insurance, and annuities. If you have named a beneficiary on any of those assets, then the beneficiary owns the asset the minute you die.

Other types of legal ownership include payable on death (POD), transfer on death (TOD), and in trust for (ITF). An account with these designations would immediately pass to the other person named on the account immediately upon your death and therefore pass outside the probate estate. This could defeat the intent of your will. Unfortunately, this happens all the time.

Many people think that this is the way to get around probate and simplify things, but that is not always the case. For example, say you are married and you are in a car accident. You die, and your spouse is listed as beneficiary or payee on death on your assets. When you die, she gets those assets immediately. That might be exactly what you intended. However, what if your wife was driving and caused the accident and the other driver was killed? You left your assets to your wife, and she inherited them immediately upon your death. However, now all those assets are subject to a lawsuit from the heirs of the other person who died.

Let's look at another twist on this example. Your wife is driving and hits a tree. You are killed, but your wife survives. Unfortunately, she has severe head injuries and needs nursing home care for the rest of her life. All of those assets that you had designated to her specifically outside of probate immediately became hers and are now subject to claims by the nursing home in order to provide for her care. Again, this is not what you intended.

In another example, let's say you have a wife and three children. You have three bank accounts with a different child named as a beneficiary on each one. If you die in a car accident, your wife, who survived you, is not going to get any of the money out of those three bank accounts because they were immediately payable to your children, even though your will leaves everything to your wife. This is another example of an unintended consequence. We once had a client who put her two adult children on her accounts. She came home from vacation to find that all of her bank accounts had been cleaned out by the IRS. Although she was not aware of it, her son owed back taxes to the IRS. Because his name was on her account, the IRS had access to it and took the money to satisfy the obligation. In most cases, adding someone to your accounts as a beneficiary has more risks than potential rewards.

If your goal is to pass your assets to your spouse or children, there are better ways to do so. One of the best ways to do so is to use trusts. We will talk about trusts and how to use them to your benefit in the next chapter. The examples in this chapter highlight the potential problems with threat number six, not knowing your predators and creditors.

Chapter 5

What Is a Trust and Why Use

Trust-Based Planning?

A trust is a legal entity that you create, much like setting up a corporation. A trust is a document that sets up a legal entity that can then own property. Property placed into a trust is then owned by the trust itself and not by the individual.

There are two general groups of trusts and then various types within each group. An inter vivos or living trust is a trust that you set up while you are still alive. The second group is a testamentary trust, which is set up through your will. A living trust can be used to manage assets during your lifetime. A testamentary trust can only manage assets after your death because the will that creates the testamentary trust does not go into effect until you pass away.

There are two types of living trusts: revocable and irrevocable. A trust is much like having a piggybank when you were a child. Some of those piggybanks had the slot in the top to put the money in, but they also had a hole in the bottom that allowed you to get the money out at your discretion. That is a revocable trust. An irrevocable trust is like a piggybank that only had the slot to put the money in but no hole in the bottom for you to take it out.

There are many advantages to using trusts to manage your assets. You can be the trustee, which is the person who manages the trust. You can determine who gets what assets and can change those determinations at any time. If one of your beneficiaries or relatives does something you do not like, you can change the terms of the trust. You can set conditions on when your beneficiaries do and do not get assets from the trust. You can also get income from the trust. Both types of trusts allow you to manage assets during your lifetime. However, any asset you put into a revocable trust can be removed from the trust at your discretion. In an irrevocable trust, once you put an asset into the trust, you cannot remove it for your own benefit; although you can receive income from the trust. An irrevocable trust is used for asset protection and VA and Medicaid planning.

The advantage to using an inter vivos trust is that any assets you have in trust do not have to go through probate at the time of your death. Because the trust itself owns the asset, it is not necessary to probate a will to transfer those assets. In the trust itself, you set up beneficiary designations naming the people who are to get the assets in the trust after your death.

Probate is a very lengthy and public proceeding in which all of your information about your estate is public record at the probate office in the county where you reside. With a trust, that information can remain private, and no one knows what assets you had at the time of your death or how they were distributed. One additional advantage of an irrevocable trust is that your creditors and other predators cannot access the assets. Therefore, if you get sued, the creditor cannot access the asset because you have no ownership in the asset itself.

This is especially beneficial if you have to go into a nursing home. Because the asset is owned by an irrevocable trust and you give up the right to access the asset, neither the nursing home nor medicaid have the right to the assets in the trust. This is one of the most popular ways of planning for nursing home care and protecting assets for your loved ones. The important distinction to remember is that because you can access and take assets out of a revocable trust, your creditors also have access to those assets. They do not have access to the assets in an irrevocable trust because you (theoretically) do not own it either. Historically, irrevocable trusts were used solely for tax planning to help people avoid the gift and estate taxes. However, 99.7 percent of the population these days is not going to have an issue with gift and estate taxes because the personal exemption is still over $5 million per person and $10 million for married couples.

Another advantage of using a trust whether it is a living trust or testamentary trust is that you can protect the assets that you leave to your children and other heirs from their creditors and predators. For example, if you leave a large sum of money to your married daughter outright in your will and she later divorces, your son-in-law could wind up taking half of the assets you left her. We had a case once where the family farm had to be sold because it was left to a child and became marital property, and then the child divorced and did not have the money to buy out her husband's interest. The farm had to be sold, which was not the intent of the father who left it to his daughter in the will. Also, if a child has an addiction, leaving him or her money with no discretion on how he or she may access it will only enhance the addiction, and the money will be gone quickly. If you use trusts, you can control how much money is doled out to the child and not further the addiction.

In conclusion, trust-based planning is a great way to manage your assets and avoid probate. It is also a great way to protect your assets from your creditors and predators. By setting up either a living or testamentary trust, you can be very specific about how and under what circumstances your heirs can get to the inheritance you leave them. However, it has to be done correctly, and it is much better if you have a general understanding of how it works before you engage in trust-based planning.

Chapter 6

Asset Protection: You Must Know Your Creditors and Predators

As we discussed in the last chapter, there are many creditors and predators out there who would like access to your nest egg and who are a threat to your financial security. Those predators and creditors include but are not limited to the government, nursing homes, lawsuits, and even divorce or a child who is an addict, as we mentioned in the last chapter.

One of the biggest threats to your family's nest egg and security is the government in the event you have to go into a nursing home. Currently in Alabama, nursing homes cost anywhere from $5,000 to $9,000 per month. In order for Medicaid to pay for the nursing home, you have to have less than $2,000 in assets. If you have assets in your name when you enter a nursing home, they have to be exhausted before Medicaid will begin to pay for your care. If not, you will have to use those assets to pay for your care until they are gone.

Other creditors and predators to watch for include lawsuits, the IRS, bankruptcy filings, and even family members. As previously discussed, you could lose your assets if you are victim to any of these. Without proper planning, your heirs could also lose the assets that you leave to them after you pass away. Your beneficiaries run the risk of losing assets if they get divorced after they receive an inheritance from you. Imagine that half of the money you leave your daughter goes to the son-in-law you never liked in the first place because they get divorced! If you have a child who is a spendthrift and cannot manage money, the inheritance could be gone in no time.

An irrevocable trust is one of the best ways to protect against this. The trust owns the asset, so your predators and creditors cannot access those assets. You can then use them for your benefit during your lifetime and leave them to your heirs at the time of your death. Even though you give up ownership of the actual asset, you can still control where the asset goes, who benefits from it, and receive income from any income-producing assets. Additionally, if you put your real estate into the trust, you still have the right to decide who lives there. By planning ahead, you can avoid the dangers posed by threat number three, not knowing your creditors and predators.

Chapter 7

Long-Term Care: How Will I Pay?

How to pay for long-term care is one of the biggest questions that people face as they begin to age. Long term care expenses are the costs incurred for someone to care for you as you age and need help with activities of daily living such as feeding, bathing, mobility, grooming, toileting, dressing and so forth. Those services can be provided by an individual family member or commercial care company or an institution like an assisted living facility or nursing home. There are basically only three ways to pay for long-term care:

1. You pay.

2. Your long-term care insurance policy pays.

3. The government pays.

1. **You pay:** As previously mentioned, nursing home costs run anywhere from $5,000 to $9,000 a month in Alabama. Therefore, a four-year stay in a

nursing home could cost you anywhere from $240,000 to $432,000! Private companies that provide in-home care are available but can also be expensive depending on the amount of time they spend at your home. You certainly have the right to pay out of your pocket, but it can be very expensive and can deplete the assets that your spouse may need to live on.

2.   **Your long-term care insurance policy pays:** If you had the forethought to purchase a long-term care insurance policy, then hopefully it will pay a significant portion of those nursing home expenses. Some of those policies are very good. Some include a return of premium provision where the company gives your premiums back. If you have a policy that pays $200 a day, that is $6,000 per month to cover your care. While there are some good policies on the market, there are some that have limitations. Unfortunately, most people wait too long to purchase the policies and the premiums are not affordable.

There are some newer products out there that provide asset based long term care.

3.   **The government pays:** The government under Medicaid provisions will pay for long-term care if you qualify. In order to qualify, you must have less than $2,000 in nonexempt assets and limited income. For the most part, Medicaid only pays for nursing home care. There are some waiver programs in Alabama that allow it to pay for in-home or assisted living care; however, those programs are very limited.

Fortunately, there are ways to plan ahead to protect your assets and allow Medicaid to begin paying sooner. However, at this point, Medicaid has a sixty-month look-back, which means it will look back to see if you have transferred any assets out of your name in the last sixty months. If you have done so, you will be penalized at the rate of $5,500 per month before Medicaid will begin paying for your long-term care. The sooner planning begins, obviously the better.

One other benefit that may assist you with long-term care expenses is known as VA pension or VA aid and attendance. This benefit is only available to veterans or their spouses who qualify. To do so, the veteran must have served at least ninety days active duty, with at least one day of that during an active war period. You must also meet asset-and-income criteria and be disabled according to the VA's standards. If you are over 65, you automatically meet the disability requirement. Again, with planning, you can meet the financial eligibility challenge without waiting to be destitute. Like Medicaid, you must have limited assets to qualify. Unlike Medicaid, there is no look back period if you do transfer assets and the amount of assets you can keep is more than Medicaid allows. The great thing about this benefit is that it is payable directly to you and can be used for in-home care or assisted living, not just for nursing home care.

The sad news is that only about 5 percent of all eligible veterans are receiving this benefit. Why? The basis for qualification is very confusing, and the Veterans Administration staff is overworked and does not tell people everything they need to know about qualifying.

The VA pension program is not an income-based program; it is a needs-based program. The program is designed to help you offset the costs of long-term care by providing a tax-free monthly benefit to cover any recurring monthly medical expenses you incur. Therefore, whether you qualify is not really based on your income, it is based on your income after recurring long term care expenses are deducted. Those expenses include costs for medical care as well as care giver expenses for in home care or the costs of an assisted living facility.

In addition to veterans, some qualifying widows are also available for the benefit. The amount of the benefit depends on level of need, but at this point, the maximum benefit available to veterans is over $25,000 per year and is tax-free.

If you are a veteran or veteran widow and have recurring monthly medical expenses and/or are receiving assistance with your activities of daily living (such as bathing, dressing, cooking, etc.), we urge you to contact us so we can determine whether you qualify for this underused benefit that you worked hard to earn.

There is an application process, but only certain qualified people including attorneys accredited by the VA can assist you. No one can charge you for filing an application. We do charge for the pre-planning that goes into getting you qualified to receive the benefit and can discuss this with you if you like. We do not charge for the intitial consultation where you will find out whether you do qualify.

Chapter 8

Applying for Medicaid

One of the first considerations in a Medicaid application is to be sure that the applicant qualifies. Many strategies can be implemented to help you become qualified for Medicaid without waiting sixty months. As mentioned previously, sixty months is the period that Medicaid will look back to see if any assets have been transferred for less than fair-market value. This prohibits you from giving your assets away as gifts to your children just so that you can qualify. You can give your assets away if you choose, but Medicaid will penalize you. However, the penalty period has nothing to do with sixty months. Many people (including attorneys) get confused about this concept. Let's consider some examples.

Tom is seventy years old and has been concerned for a while that he might have to go into a nursing home. On March 1, 2010, he gave his daughter $110,000 as a gift. Unfortunately, on July 1, 2014, he had to go into a nursing home. Medicaid will decline to pay for his care upon his initial application because he gave away assets within the past sixty months. Before Medicaid will begin paying, Tom or his family will have to pay the nursing home for twenty months ($110,000 divided by $5,500). The $5,500 is the monthly divisor that Medicaid in Alabama currently uses.

Let's now assume that Tom does not have to go into the nursing home until February 1, 2015. Even though it has been fifty-nine months since the transfer was made, the same analysis and result that was reached in the first example is reached here, even though he is only one month from qualifying. Tom would still have to pay for 20 months! However, if Tom waits two months until April 1, 2015, to apply, then Medicaid would begin to pay immediately because he has not made any uncompensated transfers within the last sixty months. The last transfer was sixty-one months ago. By waiting two more months, he reduces his penalty to zero.

Finally, assume Tom gave the money away on March 1, 2010, and then applied for Medicaid on April 1, 2010. Even though it has only been one month, Tom is still only penalized based on the amount he gave away, $110,000. Therefore, he would have to pay the nursing home himself for twenty months before Medicaid would begin to pay.

As mentioned previously, many strategies can be used to minimize the penalty period and the amount that is at risk to Medicaid in the event you or a loved one has to go into a nursing home. Every situation is different. We do a comprehensive analysis of our client's situation and put our recommendations in writing.

Once you are qualified for Medicaid, the application can be very difficult to fill out and get filed. Local Medicaid offices have their own rules and regulations that they follow. Without knowing those rules and regulations, the application may be delayed. Every month of delay costs an additional $5,000 to $9,000, depending on the cost of nursing home care in your area. We have helped many families whose loved one was already in the nursing home save on nursing home costs by doing a proper plan for them. Instead of using all of your assets to pay for care, you might very well be able to cut your losses. We can help you do so. With proper planning, you can debunk many of the myths that are perpetuated about Medicaid and the nursing home. Unfortunately, these myths prevent most people from seeking advice about the law as it applies to them. With planning, you can avoid threat number two, not knowing the law you think you know.

Chapter 9

Other Issues

1. **Special-needs planning**: Specific planning strategies are available if you have a special-needs child. This is true whether the child is a minor or an adult with a disability. Legal documents known as special-needs trusts can be set up to manage money for the benefit of these special-needs children. The advantage of having a properly drafted special-needs trust is that it can be used to pay for things other than food and shelter, which is what government benefits pay for. The special-needs trust can be set up to provide for extra care for your disabled loved one. Without the special-needs trust, the disabled loved one could lose the government benefits if he or she is given extra money or benefits.

2. **Personal care plans**: One of the additional things we offer as part of our planning process is a very specific

personal care plan. When you go into a nursing home, most of them are understaffed. They certainly will provide for your needs, but most of them do not have time to provide you with special attention. In our trust documents, we can include a personal care plan that makes the trustee responsible for making sure that you receive additional services that others won't receive. For example, you could request that you get your hair done once a week, be taken outside for at least an hour every day or longer on the weekends, or receive subscriptions to specific magazines. You can specify when or if you want visitors, what kinds of food you do and do not want to be served and what kind of TV programming you would like to watch. Plans are specific to you and designed to provide for your care and comfort in a more specialized way until you pass away.

3.   **Trust funding:** If you elect to use trusts in your planning, whether for asset protection or to avoid probate, we can provide you with directions as to how to fund the assets into the trust, an indispensable step in

making your plan effective. We can work with your financial advisor or we can handle the funding of your trust documents if you prefer. Whichever way you choose to go, it is essential that the assets be transferred to the trust in order to protect them properly.

Chapter 10

Why Miller Estate and Elder Law?

Elder law, estate planning and Medicaid planning and applications are very complicated areas of law. We are part of a nationwide network of attorneys who share information and strategies. We have attended multiple conferences across the country to learn about this specialized area of the law. We also use state-of-the-art software to analyze your situation and advise you on what you need to do to carry out your wishes and how much money you can save if you do ever have to go into a nursing home.

Additionally, we like to work with your accountant and financial advisor to implement your plan. It is important that all of your trusted advisors be involved and agree on what is best for you and your family. Your financial advisor is primarily concerned with maximizing your portfolio, and your accountant is concerned with minimizing taxes. Our main concern is protecting your assets from the government/Medicaid in the event that you have to go into a nursing home. Sometimes those three objectives are not consistent. However, if that is the case, your advisors should be willing to put your concerns and objectives first, not our own concerns. Having all of your advisors work together for your benefit will give you the confidence you need to make the right decisions.

In addition to having your advisors present, we also encourage you to bring your family members to your meetings. It is important that those close to you be involved in decisions of this magnitude. Ultimately, you will decide what is most important to you. We have plans that range from very basic wills to more sophisticated asset protection plans involving multiple trusts. There is no way to know what is right for you without educating you on these issues, learning your goals and objectives, and allowing you to choose which plan suits your needs.

We are not in the business of selling documents. LegalZoom can handle that. We are in the business of providing solutions that are tailored to your wishes. LegalZoom cannot do that. The worst thing that can happen is that you get a will from LegalZoom and think you are protected only to find out that those documents did not help you. We also have maintenance plans that provide you with unlimited telephone access, changes to your plan, and updates in the event the law changes. You become a client for life if you choose to do so!

Miller Estate and Elder Law Workshop

Attend one of our free ***The 7 Biggest Mistakes People Make in Estate Planning and How to Avoid Them*** workshops, where you will learn

- why putting a loved one's name on your account has more risks than rewards;

- why your advanced medical directive may not be adequate to carry out your end-of-life wishes;

- strategies you can implement to prevent the nursing home from taking all of your assets;

- Why a trust may be better than a will for distributing your assets at your death;

- the three documents everyone should have, regardless of their assets or income level; and

- why your own family members can be the biggest threat to your assets.

Call us at **256-241-6794** to register for one of our upcoming workshops, or go to www.MillerEstateAndElderLaw.com to learn more.

Made in the USA
Columbia, SC
28 July 2023